be
BOLD

be
BOLD

Interiors for the brave of heart

EMILY HENSON

photography Catherine Gratwicke

rps

RYLAND PETERS & SMALL
LONDON • NEW YORK

Senior designer Toni Kay
Senior commissioning editor
  Annabel Morgan
Location research Jess Walton
Head of Production Patricia Harrington
Art director Leslie Harrington
Editorial director Julia Charles
Publisher Cindy Richards

First published in 2018 by
Ryland Peters & Small
20–21 Jockey's Fields,
London WC1R 4BW
and
341 East 116th Street
New York, NY 10029

www.rylandpeters.com

Text copyright © Emily Henson 2018
Design and photographs copyright
© Ryland Peters & Small 2018

10 9 8 7 6 5 4 3 2 1

ISBN 978-1-78879-023-9

A CIP record for this
book is available from
the British Library.

Library of Congress CIP data
has been applied for.

Printed and bound in China

Contents

Bold is beautiful

My books seem to be growing more autobiographical with each one I write. It appears that I don't know how to write a book just about interiors because, for me, interiors and emotions and lifestyle choices are all interconnected. The way we decorate our homes directly correlates with the way we feel. Like us, they change and evolve over time. Our homes are living, breathing manifestations of what's going on in our heads and our hearts and our busy lives.

But sometimes, when we're not feeling our best version of ourselves, we need to put the cart before the horse and create a home for the way we want to feel. Sort of 'fake it till you make it'. When I first had the idea for this book, I wasn't feeling bold. I felt weak and defeated. My personal life was in turmoil and my home had become pared back and simplified as a way of dealing with a life in pieces. Very little colour, no pattern, no clutter – it was so unlike me!

The calming cocoon I created for my family was just what we needed in that moment. But as time passed, the old me began to re-emerge and I started to seek inspiration from homes with joyful patterns, gutsy colour choices and exhilarating paint treatments. I wanted to feel bold, so I sought out bold people. I noticed a return to maximalism, but executed in a modern way. I had always thought of maximalist interiors as full of stuff: knick-knacks, piles of cushions and layers of textiles. But this new maximalism was more about brave choices than excessive layering.

With each of my books, I am deeply inspired by the homes we visit, and this time was no exception. I share with you here a collection of homes where boldness is a way of life, and I hope you will be as wowed by them as I was. There isn't a 'one size fits all' bold style, so I've chosen a selection of homes to suit a variety of styles. For some homeowners, being bold is about making a statement with vivid paint on every surface and neon signs on the walls; for others, boldness lies in the details – leopard print and folksy embroidered cushions clashing on a pink sofa, or window frames painted yellow in an otherwise white wall.

This book is not about calm, quiet interiors and it is a far cry from the restrained, minimalist Scandinavian look that has been on trend for several years now. Instead, it is for the brave of heart, for those of you who have something to say and aren't afraid to shout it. So whether you already feel bold or you simply aspire to it, this book is for you. Bold really is beautiful.

Decorate like
nobody's watching

Paint it bold

By now, we all know that paint is an excellent way to reinvent a room. It's inexpensive, relatively quick and something you can do yourself with minimum skill. Look through these pages, and you will find an abundance of ideas for creating a fabulously bold home with imaginative applications of paint. From mildly daring to super dramatic, there is something for everyone. Unless, of course, you want to play it safe with calm, muted neutrals. In which case, you're reading the wrong book!

I want you to think about the colours you like and want in your life (later we can talk about adding colour and pattern in the form of textiles, furniture and accessories). Nine out of the twelve homeowners we visited for *Be Bold* have used colourful paint to customize their homes, each of them creating totally different looks. (The other three made up for the lack of bold paint treatments with some very gutsy wallpaper and furnishings.)

You can test the waters by spray-painting something small – an old lamp base or a wooden stool perhaps. Usually people get hooked on the satisfyingly immediate results and begin spraying everything in sight! Tatty old furniture or new pine flat-pack pieces can be completely transformed with a coat of bright paint.

When adding colour to your rooms, you have options. If you don't want to cover the whole room, try painting part-way up the walls and leaving the top half white. If you discover an interesting plaster finish beneath ancient wallpaper and leave this exposed, so much the better. I prefer this look to a feature wall, which has had its moment. Alternatively, you could use two different colours on a wall – either complementary or contrasting hues – to make a simple graphic block. Another option is to create a contemporary mural, using masking tape to mark out a graphic design and painting only within the taped areas.

For those of you ready to dive in at the deep end, just go for it! What's the worst thing that can happen? You won't like it and you'll have to repaint. That's not the end of the world. Choose one shade and paint everything – walls, ceilings, doors, woodwork, radiators – for an intoxicating and enveloping effect. If this sounds like too much, choose a main colour for the walls and ceiling and one or two accents for doors, shelves and so on. Bear in mind how colours in different rooms complement each other when you look from one space to the next. I don't mean they should 'match' (whatever that means), just that they should appear pleasing side by side. Notice colours that work together in fashion, nature and art, and try them at home. Navy and orange, chartreuse and bubblegum pink, and fuchsia and olive are examples of unexpected but exciting combinations. Do some research, make a moodboard and find out what evokes a positive emotional reaction.

Painting wooden floorboards isn't a new idea, but rather than opt for white, why not try something more daring? Keep in mind that if your floors are bright green, you may want to tone down the furniture, going for earthy neutrals instead of strong shades. Consider painting one area only – a graphic design can delineate a spot, rather like a rug.

Lastly, don't forget frequently overlooked areas such as the interior of kitchen cabinets, window frames and stair risers. Often they are an afterthought when decorating, getting the traditional white paint treatment. Why not think of them as another opportunity to express yourself and personalize them with colour?

OPPOSITE
Six different paint colours plus an acid yellow sofa! Daring doesn't even begin to describe this homeowner. She spent some time getting the colour combinations right before painting each individual area. The colours are bright but not offensively so, and the overall effect is a little like looking through a kaleidoscope.

ABOVE LEFT

This hallway has been painted all the same shade – Farrow & Ball's Inchyra Blue – using a matt finish on the walls and satin on the doors, woodwork/trim and staircase. Hallways often don't get a lot of light, so opt for darker shades to play up to the moodiness.

LEFT

The free-spirited designer who lives here has painted literally every surface freehand, including the doorway trim, which has received a loose scallop all the way around.

ABOVE

With floor paint and masking tape, you can create a painted 'rug'. This one was designed using a computer program, but why not choose a store-bought stencil or try something simple like stripes.

OPPOSITE

The architecture of this townhouse has been used to create a graphic painted swirl effect in the stairwell. The colours are rich and sophisticated and the design is simple yet dynamic, leading the eye up and down the staircase.

PAGE 16

Designer Patricia Bustos hand-painted this mural on her apartment wall using stencils. There is no doubt that this is a much more time-consuming and tedious technique than simply hanging wallpaper, but ultimately it is more rewarding.

PAGE 17

In her vividly decorated seaside home, Amy Exton used all the paints in the colour wheel! Here, she gives second-hand furniture a new life with a thick coat of hot pink and chartreuse paint. It's a cheap and cheerful way to brighten up your home.

OPPOSITE

An unapologetically vibrant saturated blue shade enlivens Zoe Anderson's dining area. The gleaming Tom Dixon copper pendant light and simple modern furniture balance out the boldness.

RIGHT

Kitsch is the name of the game in a corner of Amy Exton's home, with ceramic cherub planters spray-painted in jazzy colours and placed alongside a tropical mural.

Creative **DIY** Create a graphic mural by marking a design on a wall using masking tape then painting within the taped areas (below). If using more than one colour, let the first dry completely before taping over it to create new shapes.

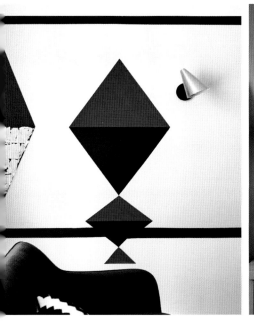

LEFT

Painting the inside of bookshelves the same colour as the walls and cabinet fronts immediately transforms an often-neglected space into a display case, framing the contents beautifully. Suddenly a casually arranged pile of books, a lamp and a simple jug of flowers look thoughtfully curated.

Pattern riot

Pattern brings me joy. I'm drawn to it wherever I go, and as a result I've managed to accumulate quite a collection of patterned 'things'. I have an embarrassingly large pile of colourful textiles in an armoire that is almost bursting at the seams. There are elaborately decorated wallpaper scraps stacked in boxes waiting for me to, what, collage a wall like it's 2002 again? And one entire side of my already small wardrobe/closet is overrun by beautiful but impractical vintage dresses that I will never wear yet can't part with. They are pretty and they make me smile, and sometimes I like to just touch them. Such is the hold pattern has on me.

Bold pattern seems to scare a lot of people with its in-your-face brashness. And while pattern isn't an essential part of a bold interior — in some of the spaces we have featured it's used sparingly, if at all — it is a powerful way to turn up the volume in a room and express your personality.

There are a number of means by which to bring pattern into your home: textiles, wallpaper, carpets and rugs, tiles, upholstery and creative paint treatments. Perhaps you're like me — drawn to a variety of different styles. My textile collection consists of vintage faded florals, kitchy retro prints, rustic striped canvas, polka dots and over-dyed neon linen, to name but a few. I like them all, but they don't necessarily work together, so it's important to edit in order to avoid visual chaos.

Learning how to mix patterns is tricky, especially if you're yearning to be bold, because daring decorating is all about breaking the rules. But, as with anything, it's good to know what the rules are, even if it's just so that you can break them. It's possible to successfully mix different designs as long as they share the same palette. Make sure your chosen patterns have three or four shades in common, then throw in a pop of colour for contrast. It's essential to break up the riot of pattern with some solid blocks of colour for visual respite — add an unpatterned textile, paint or piece of furniture in one of your main shades.

Wallpaper is an obvious way of introducing pattern, but consider alternative places to apply it. Personally, I love a wallpapered wardrobe/armoire door — it's unexpected and very useful if you rent. You might not be allowed to paper the walls, but you can do what you want with your IKEA closet, right? On photo shoots we often use 'flats', which are fake walls. You could create something similar at home with a large piece of cheap plywood. Covered in wallpaper, it will provide a flexible, movable expanse of pattern that can be leaned against any wall for a playful backdrop. Handy if you're a renter, or just commitment-phobic.

Patterned carpets are making a comeback, and I'm delighted. They are not for the faint of heart or for those with a low boredom threshold, as wall-to-wall decorative carpet is a bold choice. If you're not sure how you will feel about this hefty investment a year from now, then opt for patterned rugs — at least they can migrate to a different room. I heard that Kate Moss has leopard-print carpet at home and I don't doubt it. How fabulous is that?

Pictured on these pages are some extreme examples of pattern clash, but if you want to take baby steps to being bold (isn't that a contradiction in terms?), start small with brightly decorated cushions on a plain sofa or vivid patterned curtains in an otherwise calm room. Or you can just go for it, like these fearless souls have.

OPPOSITE
In a Paris penthouse, the homeowner's daring style is let loose in her dressing room, where the walls are lined with custom-built wardrobes/closets upholstered in Matthew Williamson's Sunbird fabric. Some might have stopped there, but she took it a step further, adding wall-to-wall pink banana leaf-print carpet, which works brilliantly against all the odds.

PAGE 22
In the eating area of a Madrid apartment, the right-hand wall is covered in an abstract floral wallpaper by Jessica Zoob and the left in large-scale Moroccan tile, neither patterns nor colours linking in an obvious way. The reupholstered vintage chairs echo the shades of the wallpaper, while the Moroccan rug and palm-print lampshade add yet more detail to this confident, layered look.

PAGE 23
Glossy blue and green cabinets are sleek and sophisticated, but the patterned floor tiles injects a playful note into this kitchen. The haphazard arrangement of colour and pattern is charming.

LEFT
In this child's room, an oversized pink poppy wallpaper is paired with a black and white starburst curtain. There's no reason why it should work, but it does.

ABOVE
Earth tones accented with pink and gold link different patterns in the bedroom of designer Anna Hayman. The block colour of the orange faux fur throw offers a moment of visual respite.

OPPOSITE
On the spacious landing of a Parisian townhouse, custom-built wardrobes/closets are covered in a magical botanical paper, Kvitter by Hanna Werning.

LEFT
The homeowners laid these decorative Moroccan tiles themselves when they were unable to convince their builder to fit them in the slightly wonky, imperfect way they desired.

RIGHT
Little girls' rooms don't have to be sugary sweet. Fairies and unicorns are fabulous, but if you're investing in wallpaper, it's wiser to choose a design that will carry your daughter through to later years. This large-scale poppy design is enchanting, especially when balanced with plain bed linen.

Creative **DIY**
Steal a trick used on photo shoots and create your own 'flat' at home (opposite). Essentially it is a fake wall, a large piece of plywood covered in wallpaper to create a movable backdrop. Here, two 'flats' lean against the wall in a dining room, each covered in a different Cole & Son wallpaper, to be brought out depending on the owner's mood.

Make a statement

Painting your interiors orange and pink or layering them with clashing patterns aren't the only ways to create a bold statement at home. And making a statement is really what this book is all about – telling the world, or at least those people who cross your threshold, "this is me". It is your opportunity to do things exactly the way you want.

Think about your furniture for a minute. Chances are, like most of us, your sofa is a neutral shade – grey, brown or navy blue. What would happen if you decided not to play it safe? I'm long overdue a new sofa, my current (grey) one having seen better days, and I've promised myself that next time I will be more daring. I think we worry that if we opt for large pieces of furniture in bright colours, we will be committed to a particular scheme for years and tire of it. Of course, this is a possibility, and I appreciate that a sofa is a big-ticket item. But what if that one bold move is exactly what you need to bring your home to life?

Over the years I've met people who have invested in furniture in daring and unusual shades, and none of them – I promise – have ever expressed regret. If anything, it seems to empower them to embrace the spirit of bold living even more. But bold doesn't have to mean bright. You could choose pale pink, sage green, aquamarine – anything but the obvious. If the thought of a brightly coloured sofa makes you uneasy, try an armchair. A vibrant upholstered chair like the orange example on page 33 is

one of those things that simultaneously goes with nothing and everything, rather like leopard print in fashion. You just need one standout piece that your guests will be drawn to, in awe of your adventurous spirit.

Similarly, wardrobes/armoires with hand-painted or carved designs are so much more interesting than plain wood. I have a red Chinese armoire painted with butterflies that we bought when living overseas 15 years ago. It's not really my style any more, and it doesn't go with anything else I have, but I still love it for its boldness (and of course for the story it tells). This goes back to the age-old interiors advice that if you buy what you love, you'll find a way to make it work. And if what you love is a neon yellow velvet chair, I'm here to say go right ahead!

Some other ways to make a statement: group large, expressive pieces together to create a sense of theatre. A mural, an oversized floor lamp and an albino peacock may not have much in common, but when arranged in a cluster they become a work of art. Look at your collections (translation: the random stuff you own) to see what can be styled together to make an interesting 'story'. The aim is to create a moment of unexpected drama, so think about using materials in different ways. Paint your stair risers eye-catching colours or wallpaper them. Stairs are often the first thing people see when they enter a front door, so why not make them into a feature? Add ceramic tiles to living room walls instead of just the bathroom; use coloured grout in your tilework instead of the usual white; layer colour on colour – put a red chair in front of a red wall.

Allowing yourself to be bold can be scary. It takes courage and confidence, and you have to let go of the fear of being judged, but sometimes it's important to fake bravery until you really feel it. And if you can't express your true self in your own home, then where can you? Your home is your canvas and the statements you make paint a picture of who you are, so say it loud and proud.

OPPOSITE
Enter this cottage in the British countryside and you're greeted by a wildly original staircase. Designer Anna Hayman used a width of her Pearl wallpaper on the stair treads, adding more painterly details to the woodwork and walls. This loose style of painting takes confidence to pull off, but the beauty is in the imperfection.

ABOVE
In an elegant sitting room on the outskirts of Paris, design classics nestle around the extraordinary chimney breast. Treated with a metal coating designed by L'Atelier du Mur, the ombre-effect finish fades from oxidized brass to polished brass to muted zinc. The seriousness of the Eames lounge chair and the Noguchi by Vitra coffee table is lightened by the tiger rug by Moustache.

LEFT
In The Hague, a designer couple have embraced their small, dark bedroom by painting it a rich velvety green and layering the bed with dark linens, most of them from Dutch brand By Mölle. The vivid yellow cushion is by Hay.

OPPOSITE
Encaustic cement tiles have been used on the floor and to line a section of the wall in this Parisian kitchen, creating a dramatic backdrop for the linen sofa. With so many beautifully designed tiles available now, consider using them as you would wallpaper or paint. The sofa is a custom design created by Anne Geistdoerfer of Double G.

PAGE 32

Dutch designer Pien Essink's studio was painted a warming raspberry paint for a photo shoot and she decided to keep the colour. An adventurous spirit, rather than opting for something neutral to set against the cheerful hue, she chose red vintage cinema chairs in a slightly different shade and a vintage botanical print.

PAGE 33

Matt black painted walls, charcoal floorboards and a smoky glass mirror are quietly moody and elegant. Adding the iconic Mushroom armchair by Pierre Paulin in a fiercely bold orange wool immediately turns up the volume in this stylish Dutch home. Be daring when it comes to upholstered chairs – a single armchair in a brilliant colour energizes an entire room.

ABOVE LEFT

This is one idea that I am definitely stealing for my next home. I fell in love with the simple yet wonderfully effective use of materials in this London kitchen. The pink tile isn't expensive, but when it's laid herringbone style and finished with yellow grout, it is so much more than the sum of its parts. Grout comes in a multitude of colours now, so why do we default to white? I dare you to opt for the unexpected.

ABOVE RIGHT

Another example of punchy statement seating, the ergonomic Ekstrem chair by Terje Ekstrom is surprisingly comfy, its arms and legs hugging the sitter. Consider adding a neon light to make your own statement – Patricia Bustos wrote her chosen words, then had them made in neon.

OPPOSITE

One corner of an open-plan kitchen/dining room is transformed into a carefully curated moment by grouping unusual large-scale pieces in front of a pastoral mural. The Muffin lamp is by Brokis and similar murals can be found at Surface View.

OPPOSITE

Sometimes all a room needs is one standout piece. In this bright Dutch home, white walls and polished concrete floors dominate the ground floor. But instead of going down the industrial, pared-back route, eclectic and unusual pieces of furniture have been peppered throughout, this folksy, hand-painted armoire being just one example.

BELOW

The surest way to a satisfyingly strong look is to limit your colour palette – something I've said again and again. In this child's playroom, the dynamic zigzag rug is the starting point for the scheme – the colours for the walls, the armchair and the floor cushion are all pulled from its palette.

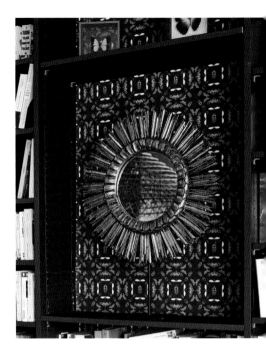

Creative **DIV** *In a bold home, every last inch of space offers an opportunity to express yourself. Here, one part of a bookcase has been lined with wallpaper, left empty and dressed with a sunburst gilt mirror (above). A similar effect can be achieved using individual sheets of decorative paper from specialist stationery stores pasted to walls – particularly useful for smaller areas that don't require much paper.*

More is more

This might sound like an odd analogy, but hear me out. I don't have any tattoos, but I love them on other people and many of my friends are covered in them. Have you noticed that most people with lots of tattoos don't seem to regret them? The more they have, the less it becomes about one individual design being good or bad, relevant or dated. Instead, the whole picture, the collection itself, tells a story about who the person is, where he or she once lived and their interests at certain points in their lives. Their skin is a living, breathing, evolving storybook that's all about them.

I believe that this is how we should think of our homes. They should reveal who we are, how we like to live and the things that make us feel good. As an incurable maximalist, I struggle with homes that don't have much in them, mostly because they don't tell me anything about the people who live there. While I'm not advocating becoming a hoarder (or having tattoos, for that matter), I do think that our possessions have a great deal to say about who we are. There is a fine line between cool maximalism and claustrophobic clutter, and of course the threshold for that line is different for everyone, but for a boldly beautiful home, more is always more.

Maximalism may go in and out of fashion, but some of us are diehard fans. It's in our blood. We can't help but pile it on; we can't stop collecting and dressing our homes in new ways. I pick up bits and pieces wherever I go, and

my job as a stylist requires that I collect these things (to be honest, it really doesn't, but it's a good excuse, so go along with me, OK?). 'More is more' doesn't have to mean hoarding a plethora of knick-knacks that will only gather dust. It can also refer to vivid colour combinations, contrasting patterns, artfully mismatched furniture and layered textures. For me, it's about creating joyful interiors that stop people in their tracks and make them look twice. I saw a woman at a bus stop the other day and she looked so utterly fabulous that I snapped a quick picture as my bus flew past. Red ballet pumps, orange tights, a pink skirt, a floral blouse under a lemon cardigan, colourful beads around her neck, a little knitted hat with flowers sewn onto it and bright pink lipstick gleaming. Even her plastic shopping bags looked like well-planned accessories. She was a hair's breadth away from looking insane (some might argue that she had already arrived), but that's what I liked. She didn't care. Her body, her clothes, her rules. She was living her best life with boldness, ease and confidence, and it was a sight to see on a dreary, rainy London day.

More is more decorating is difficult to explain because there aren't any rules. I can't promise that if you combine this colour with that pattern and this chair you'll suddenly 'get the look'. Because the look is you. It's those crazy ideas you've been too afraid to put into action for fear of getting it wrong. It's your secret desire to paint the floor mustard or the ceiling green and to reupholster your sofa with a palm-tree print. 'Getting the look' boils down to letting those ideas out, trusting your instincts and experimenting – which means getting it wrong and trying again until you have achieved the right amount of boldness for you.

Luckily with interiors – unlike tattoos – you always have the chance to edit. So that late-night decision to buy leopard-print curtains can be rectified without the pain and expense of a laser. Although why you'd ever second-guess a decision to buy leopard curtains is lost on me.

OPPOSITE
Designed with fashion photo shoots in mind, this
living room is certainly photogenic! The coral paint
sets the stage for the layering of yet more vibrant
hues. The tropical-print sofa is by Swoon, while
the graffitied canvas came from a local junk shop.
You can find similar neon lights at Seletti.

OPPOSITE & ABOVE

This homeowner follows no rules when it comes to choosing colour for her home. Very little is planned, so the grey-green walls, the yellow Ligne Roset armchair, the red vintage rug and blue paint were all part of a layering process that evolved over time. The pink side table (above) is by Pulpo.

LEFT

This room doesn't have a great deal in it yet still exudes personality, proving that, with clever use of materials, you can be a maximalist without too much clutter. Two assertive shades of paint, a graphic black and white painted 'rug', a custom-designed wooden sliding door and the acid yellow sofa are modern and sharp.

ABOVE

In this living room, Damien Hirst dots, a red rug and a gathering of ceramic ladies make for an interesting corner. The jade cabinet is by Bethan Gray at W.A. Green and the ceramics are by Jonathan Adler.

PAGE 42

This dining area is screened from the entrance to a Parisian home. One side of the angled partition walls are covered in Martinique banana leaf wallpaper, the other in wallpaper by Custhom. The dining chairs are by NV Gallery and the hall mirror is by AYTM.

PAGE 43

Anything goes in this Madrid apartment, where a bamboo tiki bar holds court with 1980s Ekstrem chairs, a mid-century marble-topped coffee table and a neon sign. What makes it work? A limited colour palette and the guts to own the look.

OPPOSITE

The first thing you see when you enter this home is this mural, hand-painted using stencils by the homeowner and her children. The grapefruit yellow sofa is a reupholstered vintage piece. The faux zebra rug takes the look from elegant to glamorous.

BELOW

These Bert & May encaustic floor tiles were an adventurous choice, as the colours don't match the painted stairs. If they had, it would look too perfect – it's the off-kilter hues that create impact.

Creative **DIY** Be on the lookout for interesting pieces to hang on your walls. Here, vintage bamboo and rattan screens have been hung very simply on L-brackets, bringing detail and interest to a mustard-painted wall and mirror (*above*).

Trailblazers

Delicately DECADENT

Walking into Patricia Bustos' Madrid apartment is like going back in time. Specifically to 1960s Palm Springs. But look a little closer and you quickly discover that this is a thoroughly modern home designed by an artist with her eyes fixed firmly on the future.

OPPOSITE
The lighting makes a statement in the dining area, where a fabulous oversized antique piece hangs above the table. Patricia loves to scour antiques stores and markets in Madrid and the rest of Europe. The rug is Kelly Wearstler for The Rug Company and the table and chairs are vintage.

ABOVE & ABOVE LEFT
Yet more attention-grabbing lighting choices. In the living room, a tall metal palm tree floor lamp (above) emits a mellow glow in the evening, while the kitchen is home to a retro-style brass lamp topped with a leafy palm-print shade (above left).

I wouldn't usually describe the way a homeowner looks, especially not a woman, as I don't want to contribute to society's obsession with appearances. But I will make an exception here, purely because Patricia suits her home so fantastically (or does her home suit her?). She's glamorous, elegant and colourful, yet still playful and approachable.

Be BOLD

Ceramic tiles are often used in hallways, kitchens and bathrooms. They're easy to clean, so it makes sense to fit them in hard-working areas. But travel abroad, and decorated tiles can be found throughout the home, even covering the walls. With so many striking designs on offer, it seems a shame to hide them away. These ones were designed by Patricia and handmade in Morocco.

OPPOSITE
In the open-plan kitchen/diner, Patricia built an informal seating area, a relaxed place for the family to chill over a long weekend breakfast. None of the patterns match here but somehow it all works, loosely linked by a muted colour scheme broken up by a shot of emerald green. The chairs are vintage and were reupholstered for a design show. The wallpaper is by Jessica Zoob.

Interior designer Patricia seems poised for greatness. At different points in her career she studied business, fashion design and interior design, each discipline building on the other, so she is now running a successful venture with a business savvy not always possessed by creatives. She spent many years at Spanish brand Zara designing kids' fashion before retraining as an interior designer and partnering with two friends. Now she has branched out on her own with Patricia Bustos Studio and has her sights set on nothing less than interiors world domination!

When she's designing residential homes, Patricia likes to work with her clients from the beginning of the project to the very end, advising on absolutely everything from the structural layout to the positioning of the light switches and choosing cushions. She also designs many pieces especially for clients, including sofas, sideboards and chandeliers (she has a particular fondness for lighting), and aspires to her own line of home products in the future. Patricia's particular skill lies in combining styles from different eras to create something fresh and modern.

With almost entirely white furnishings, the formal living room is the most subdued space in the apartment. The cool monochrome scheme is dotted with aquamarine flourishes, inspired by a curvy velvet sofa designed by Patricia. The art and quirky accessories prevent the room from feeling sedate and keep it in line with the tongue-in-cheek mood of the rest of the flat.

KATE MOSS

In 2018, she won first prize for her
design for Madrid's Casa Decor
exhibition; a psychedelic-glam 'Rebel
Kitchen', all pinks, greens and brass, and
a bold expression of Patricia's true style.

Patricia's apartment is not only a
family home but also her design studio
and unofficial showroom. The place was
humming with activity when I visted,
with assistants buzzing around working
on various projects. Patricia lives here
with husband Nacho, a banker, and their
three children; a four-year-old son, also
Nacho, and daughters Bella and Maya,
aged six and nine.

Something I appreciate about
Patricia's home is the way each space
feels very different to the next. Except
for the shared colour palette (teal and

shades of pink and yellow), each room
has its own distinct personality. The
hallway boasts a mural hand-painted by
Patricia and her children, and a vintage
sofa reupholstered in lemon yellow.
In the sitting room, the mood becomes
more sophisticated, with low sofas in
white linen and turquoise velvet, and
dazzling accessories in brass, coral and
ceramic. Continue to the dining room,
and the mood changes once again. On
one side of the room, a velvet loveseat
designed by Patricia in three toning
shades of pink is flanked by a pair of
wood and leopard-print cabinets, also
her own design. On the opposite side is
a retro tiki-style bar, two mustard 1980s
lounge chairs and a vibrant pink neon
sign based on Patricia's handwriting.

It's all fabulously OTT and conjures up images of wild cocktail parties with music blaring out from the pink Crosley record player in the corner.

Patricia is constantly rearranging her home, moving around her possessions and transforming the rooms. I recommend doing this every once in a while, to stop things from feeling stale. A revamp can be as simple as changing your cushion covers, or as labour intensive as rethinking the furniture layout.

For Patricia, being bold means combining different eras, ignoring outdated rules about pattern and colour matching, and injecting humour and quirkiness into everything she designs. Her home is a joyful and ever-changing expression of what's in her head, and it's fabulous.

ABOVE

The apartment is spacious enough to afford Patricia a home office from which to run her design business. The artwork that hangs behind her desk was originally part of the room that Patricia designed for Madrid's Casa Decor show in 2018.

RIGHT

In her dressing room, Patricia has again repurposed some pieces designed for the 2017 Casa Decor show. The walls are covered in a textured paper with marble and brass strips spliced in, transforming what could have been a featureless corner. She also designed the acrylic and faux fur chair.

OPPOSITE

The couple's bedroom is a calmer affair. One wall is covered in a pale geometric wallpaper by Casamance and the bed is dressed mostly in white. A mustard throw, custom-made cushions and the pink lion print by Mexican artist Paul Fuentes add flashes of colour.

OPPOSITE

The creative couple designed and built their own dining table after struggling to find one that they liked, finishing it with deep plum-coloured paint. Masters when it comes to the use of colour, they painted the walls chalky pink and the chimney breast matt black, leading to sage green and navy in the sunroom beyond.

ABOVE LEFT & RIGHT

To the left of the chimney breast hangs a gallery of the couple's art, including a striking drawing by Monika Peterson. Resting larger pieces on the floor is a looser, more relaxed way of styling a gallery wall. A shot of grass green from an oversized vintage glass lamp brightens the corner.

Colour-block
PARTY

When a couple with backgrounds in graphic design and interior architecture create a home together, you can expect an interesting result, and the elegant apartment of Theo-Bert Pot and Jelle van de Schoor in The Hague doesn't disappoint. Richly painted walls punctuated by carefully chosen furnishings and an eclectic yet sophisticated mix of accessories make this home a study in strong but subdued styling.

OPPOSITE

There is very little pattern in this home, but where it exists, it is big and – you guessed it – bold! A lightweight piece of plywood was covered in wallpaper and leans casually against a wall. The large scale of the design works well when it covers a small area. The orange velvet cushions add a luscious hit of colour to the traditional pattern of the wallpaper.

ABOVE LEFT & RIGHT

A small selection of the couple's extensive earthenware collection can be seen on a kitchen shelf. I love the contrast between the inky black walls and the wonkiness of some of the glazes.

LEFT

The kitchen was installed by Theo-Bert and Jelle at minimum cost, since this is a rented apartment. They painted the work surface green-grey and added dark grey curtains to hide the refrigerator and other kitchen clutter.

The couple met while studying at the Royal Academy of Arts in The Hague and have lived together for almost nine years now, six of those in this building near the city centre, which dates back to 1905. Luckily the creative pair share a similar taste in interiors and seem to agree harmoniously about most things. How lucky – and how rare!

The apartment isn't huge, but it feels bigger than it is, thanks to the 3.2m-/10ft-tall ceilings and a sunroom that leads out onto a good-sized garden. And what the interior lacks in space, it makes up for in character and original features – there are two fireplaces, marble floors in the entryway, attractive cornicing/

crown molding, and stained-glass windows. These details are all the more appealing when juxtaposed with strong modern shades on the walls and a mix of furniture – old, new and handmade.

When the couple moved in, the walls were white and yellow, so they set about injecting some colour with a brave use of paint, going dark in most rooms and choosing pale pink for the dining room. They decided to paint even though the apartment is rented and say that when it is time to move out they will enlist the help of their friends and repaint it. If you rent, bear in mind that you can customize your space easily and cheaply with a coat of paint – a worthwhile job if you plan to stay long term.

Jelle is an interior architect running his own studio, Form Makers, designing restaurants, bars and homes, while Theo-Bert runs graphic design studio Pot & van der Velden with his friend Isabel. Theo-Bert has been interested in interiors since childhood, painting his bedroom multiple times and helping his parents style the table for their Sunday dinners. Now he flexes his interiors muscles by decorating his own home and writing popular interiors blog The Nice Stuff Collector – an appropriate name for a man who loves to collect wherever he travels. Theo-Bert says it's a bad idea for him and Jelle to go anywhere with an empty car because it will definitely come back full.

Be **BOLD**

An inexpensive, quick and easy way to add a hit of juicy colour is with textiles. The sunroom's earthy colours and textures are boosted by the addition of brightly hued velvet cushions. The textured sofa, muted walls and sheepskin rugs offer a neutral but interesting foundation upon which to layer cushions in shades that suit the season or your mood.

The couple have few rules when it comes to what they collect, favouring a colourful yet classic aesthetic. They are just as likely to visit a local designer furniture shop to splurge on pieces by Flos, Vitra and Ligne Roset as they are to pick up vintage pieces in second-hand markets. They say they are not particularly concerned with colour or style, instead simply asking themselves "Do we both like it?" This laid-back attitude to decorating makes for a colourful and authentic home.

Something that struck me about this apartment was the use of solid blocks of strong colour on everything from the furniture, floors and walls to the cushions

OPPOSITE & RIGHT

The couple chose matt black paint for the living room walls. Dark paint scares a lot of people but can look rich and glamorous. In the daytime, light streams through the large windows so it never seems gloomy, and at night when lamps and candles are lit, the effect is moody and seductive. On the mantelpiece a stunning ceramics collection is artfully arranged to one side of the black chimney breast, with attention paid to the varying heights of each piece (opposite).

and ceramics. I've always believed that to add interest to a space you need to introduce a splash of pattern, even if it's just on a cushion or a curtain. But Jelle and Theo-Bert have proved me completely wrong, managing to create a bold, richly textured and layered home with hardly any pattern in sight. Their trick? Instead, they have used strong colour, haphazardly grouped artworks, handmade ceramics and lots of flourishing potted plants to bring their home to life.

OPPOSITE & RIGHT

A pair of low-slung Ligne Roset sofas have been upholstered in emerald velvet – a throwback to the sunken seating pits of the 1970s, an idea the couple love. Pops of orange are repeated in the gauzy terracotta curtains, the lampshade and the round orange armchair.

LEFT

The bedroom is on the small side, a fact that Theo-Bert and Jelle have embraced. Instead of choosing white paint to make it seem bigger, they opted for rich green and matt black – bold yet soothing. Layers of washed linen dress the bed and a mustard cushion shakes things up.

Psychedelic–
ON-SEA

Set designer Amy Exton might just be the poster child for the extreme end of the *Be Bold* movement. With a daring palette and theatrical eye, Amy indulges her love of colour and kitsch with no holds barred, creating a home that packs a punch from the minute you walk through the door.

ABOVE LEFT & RIGHT
No surface has been left unpainted in Amy's vibrant home. The entrance hall is electric blue – walls, doors, trim, banisters and stairs. On the floor are Marmoleum tiles in a pattern of Amy's own design. Upstairs it's all change, shifting to electrifying papaya and hot pink.

OPPOSITE
In the kitchen, Amy hand-painted this eye-popping mural herself, painstakingly taping off each area and alternating between stripes, leopard and solid painted sections. She continued the mouth-watering colour scheme with apple green on the walls and brightly coloured metal stools.

Amy shares her three-storey townhouse in the British seaside town of Margate, Kent, with flatmate Siobhan Hogan, a fashion designer, and Presley, a black and white Cockapoo. Built in 1902 as a convalescent home for children with tuberculosis, the building was originally home to ailing children sent to recuperate in the sea air. Amy moved from London to Margate in

Amy gutted the kitchen, knocking down a wall to create a large open-plan space where she could cook and socialize. Black and white fronts on the kitchen cabinets offer a moment of calm in the otherwise energizing space. Basic white tiles are grouted with black, creating a strong grid against the bright green wall. The island serves as an additional seating area and provides storage beneath.

2016 and hasn't had much time to take in that healthy sea air herself yet. With walls covered in magnolia paint and wall-to-wall brown carpet on the floors, Amy had her work cut out for her. But on day one she tore up the carpet and set to work transforming the drab interior into a candy-coloured utopia.

A fine art student first at Brighton and then at London's Central Saint Martins, Amy specialized in sculpture and installation, creating tactile and immersive pieces. Upon graduation, she was asked to recreate her degree show installation – a 5m-/16ft-high cuboid made from foil curtains – for a music video. And so her career was launched, creating sets for fashion shoots, music videos and advertisements in her signature gutsy style. When she bought this house, Amy realized she could combine her design skills with her passion for interiors and hatched a plan to design a home that would double as a location for photography and video shoots.

Before she could dive into the fun part of decorating, Amy had to tackle a few larger projects, namely a new bathroom and kitchen.

OPPOSITE
The upstairs living room is Amy's favourite room. The coating of coral paint is bright, but also surprisingly cosy and calming. There are three sofas here, each one very different. The pink sofa was found on Etsy, the Ercol on Shpock (the boot fair app and an alternative to eBay) and the third, a tropical-print boxy number (see page 39), is from Swoon. The lion painting was a junk-shop find.

ABOVE
On the landing, a vintage chair has been covered in shaggy faux fur. Next to it is a ceramic pedestal and plant pot spray-painted glossy pink. Ceramic pieces are easy to find in charity shops/thrift stores and can be updated with a coat of paint.

LEFT
Spray-paint strikes again, here on a bird lamp base that's been topped with a fringed shade. The arrow cutouts were found in a junk shop.

You can't get bolder than this! The coral paint takes on an incredibly vibrant tone behind this knockout display cabinet by DUSX. Inspired by Art Deco designs but updated in vivid green mock-croc, it is the statement piece to end all statement pieces.

Structurally there wasn't a great deal to do, but she pulled down a wall to create a large eat-in kitchen/diner. A keen cook, Amy wanted a space where she could entertain and throw open the French doors to the courtyard. In the rest of the house, the wooden floors were sanded, hallways were tiled with linoleum squares and every inch was painted shades of coral, cobalt, fuchsia, apple green and orange – a total regeneration.

Margate has had its own regeneration in recent years, with many Londoners moving here, lured by cheaper property, a high-speed rail link and skies said by painter William Turner to be the loveliest in Europe. I spent my teen years living here, and back then it definitely wasn't cool! Now, the harbour and refurbished Dreamland amusement park are teeming with creative types and the lanes are packed with vintage shops selling furniture, clothes and homewares. Much of Amy's furniture has been sourced from

PAGE 76 & 77

In her bedroom, Amy has gone for big blocks of colour on the walls and furniture, layering pattern in the bedding and rug. The antique bed may be formal in style, but that's where tradition ends. A second-hand wooden armoire has been painted chartreuse, a colour picked up in some of the bedding. The blue bedside cabinet is from IKEA.

local second-hand shops, many pieces receiving a colour-block makeover. Lamp bases, wardrobes/armoires, plant pots and even a bust of Elvis (Amy's prize possession) have all benefitted from a glossy lick of boldly coloured paint.

Because the house operates as a location, Amy has avoided too many knick-knacks, focusing instead on large paintings, furniture and props – pieces that don't get lost when photographed. Her decorating mantra is 'Think big and just go for it'. Nowhere is this more evident than in her living room, where a bright green Art Deco-style cabinet sits against a coral wall, sharing the space with three different sofas (pale pink, leopard and tropical print), a kitsch painting of a lion and a huge graffitied canvas.

Amy uses her home and business as a blank canvas where she can experiment with new ideas. Now that the house is almost entirely finished, she is thinking about starting all over again. Partly because she gets bored easily and is constantly flooded with new ideas, and partly because the brands who shoot in her home are always looking for fresh new looks.

Maybe taking bold to the extreme isn't your thing. Do you prefer your Elvis busts au naturel rather than hot pink, and your leopard prints separate from tropicals? Some might agree. Embrace instead the spirit with which Amy decorates her home and the impulsive, 'go bold or go home' attitude that permeates every corner. As she so rightly states, if you don't like it, you can always change it.

Be **BOLD**

Who says bathrooms must be calming spa-like sanctuaries? They can also be lively and stimulating, somewhere you can feel energized and inspired. By day this is a joyful sight – hot pink, strawberry and candyfloss paint are tempered only slightly by the marble-effect tiles – and by night candlelight brings out the warmth in the scheme.

Playfully
BOLD

This Victorian terraced house on a quiet street in West London has recently seen some exciting changes. It is the first property that Rachel and Chris Roberts and their young family have been able to make truly their own, redesigning it top to bottom with the help of Office S&M, an architectural firm they commissioned to create a stylish, child-friendly home.

ABOVE LEFT
The entryway and stairs immediately hint at the bold styling within this home. The stairs are painted in Farrow & Ball Inchyra Blue plus a lighter blue accent shade, while the banister gets a coat of Babouche, again by Farrow & Ball. The handrail ends in a marble sphere and the encaustic floor tiles are by Bert & May.

ABOVE & OPPOSITE
Simple materials have impact when treated in original ways. Pink tiles look fresh when laid herringbone style and finished with yellow grout. The oak-fronted cabinets are painted in Farrow & Ball Green Smoke. The bamboo and plastic Grain pendant lights are by Muuto.

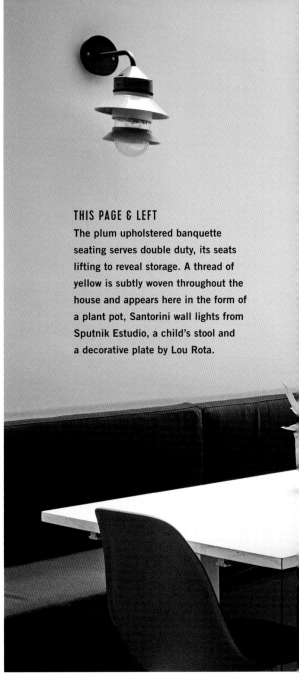

THIS PAGE & LEFT
The plum upholstered banquette seating serves double duty, its seats lifting to reveal storage. A thread of yellow is subtly woven throughout the house and appears here in the form of a plant pot, Santorini wall lights from Sputnik Estudio, a child's stool and a decorative plate by Lou Rota.

LEFT
Between the kitchen and the living room is a space where the girls can spread out their toys – which are stored handily in cupboards built into the wall – while mum has a rest on the bench (although I'm pretty certain a mum of four never rests). The adorable tiger side table is by Graham & Green, as is the embroidered cushion.

PAGES 84 & 85
At the front of the house is the living room, its walls cloaked in an intense and saturated blue from Farrow & Ball that also coats the cabinets and shelves that flank the fireplace. A black and white rug from the Plantation Rug Company, patterned silk cushions and a woven toy basket enliven the room further. The butterfly prints are from Rockett St George.

The busy professional couple – Rachel is a doctor and Chris a financial analyst – bought the house in 2013. Like many of us, their homes have always been decorated in dribs and drabs, never exactly the way they wanted. In 2016, they enlisted the help of London-based architects Office S&M to help create their dream home. At the time, the couple had three daughters and wanted to extend the loft to add another bedroom so that all the girls would have a room.

They also planned to open up the kitchen to make it more suitable for family life. Now Rachel and Chris are parents to four girls: Vesper, aged six, four-year-old twins Taylor and Celeste, and newest addition Clara, six months old. When we visited, Rachel and Clara – a gorgeous, happy baby – were our hosts, but I am assured that when all the girls are home (and there isn't a photo shoot taking place), noise levels are higher and toys are strewn everywhere.

I feel better knowing this because, as it is, the house is pretty perfect – a home that has been carefully considered and with no space wasted. Banquette seating was fitted in the kitchen, handy for stashing the aforementioned toys, while cupboards were built into the walls in the living room, filled with baskets that hold crayons, colouring books, train sets and princess dresses. With four young children, organization is key.

A strong and varied colour palette was chosen for the interior, from dark teal to flamingo pink to cerulean blue. Woven through many of the rooms is a thread of vibrant pineapple yellow. An accent colour is such an effective trick for tying together different colour palettes and it can be as simple as adding a cushion in the linking hue. In the entrance hall, the floors are laid with encaustic tiles from Bert & May, the only area to be treated to pattern. The stairs and walls are coated in various shades of teal, with that sunny yellow hue punching through on the banisters.

Be BOLD

So much space is taken up by staircases and hallways that it's a shame to waste it. Think of them as an extension of your rooms, and treat them with the same care and thought. Architects Office S&M designed this playful handrail and banister, drawing inspiration from game Snakes & Ladders. Using three different colours makes this busy, functional area into a visual feast.

OPPOSITE

On the top floor, a bedroom was added for the growing family, with three arched windows painted in a sunny yellow shade. The shutters block out the light and add a sweet charm. The walls are painted in Farrow & Ball's Calamine, a pink that is soothing rather than saccharine sweet.

The girls' bathroom is
simple and efficient yet
fun and playful. The basic
white tiles are grouted
with black, a wise choice
since white grout stains
quickly. The sink area
is laid with smaller pink
tiles, linking to the girls'
bedroom. A peppering
of that joyful yellow, via
the knobs, towels, mirror,
towel rack and even the
stool, completes the look.

Towards the back of the house is the kitchen extension, from
which I plan to steal many an idea for my own home. The colours here
are punchy but not jarring. The crisp white walls are a backdrop for sage
green cupboards, a deep plum banquette and pale pink herringbone tiles
with bright yellow grout. Finished with pops of yellow throughout,
the effect is incredibly satisfying.

Up the stairs, the teals and yellow continue until you reach the girls'
floor. One bedroom is painted a soothing pink, its rear wall punctuated
by three arched windows. Next door in the bathroom, basic white square
tiles are given added value with black grout, and yellow accessories are
dotted throughout – doorknobs, a mirror, a stool, even the heated towel
rack are all a sunny yellow shade. A smaller area of pink tile softens
and warms the look.

This home shows that when you commit to a colour palette, it pays
off. Simple ideas are elevated when linked by colour, and the luscious
tones satisfy the eye. With simple materials used in fresh, modern ways,
heaps of confident colour and a few luxurious splurges, the Roberts
have built a happy home with room for their family to grow.

OPPOSITE
Sometimes a boldly
decorated home needs to
offer a moment of respite.
For these busy working
parents, their bedroom
is that calm sanctuary,
painted in Farrow & Ball's
Mizzle. Not every room
has to be wild and
energized. You can be
bold and still want a
break from the intensity
it brings! Here, the soft
palette is accented with
a burst of juicy tangerine.

FAR LEFT & LEFT
The sofa is from French brand Caravane and was customized using three different fabrics – a textured geometric print, palest pink linen and teal velvet. Create a similar look on a budget by layering single-sized feather mattress toppers, covered in the fabric of your choice, on your sofa. More geometric shapes: squares and triangles appear on the colour-block rug, sectional table and beaded box (left).

A case of the
PARISIAN BLUES

When interior designer Anne Geistdoerfer designs for others, she considers it her mission to create a space that reflects her clients and their lifestyles perfectly. While she claims that it is more difficult to do this for herself, her Parisian townhouse paints an admirably balanced picture of family life, style, comfort and beauty. As most designers will tell you, their home is a place to try out new ideas and Anne is no exception, using all four floors to experiment.

OPPOSITE
Teal paint in the same shade as the sofa was used to cover walls, ceiling and shelves, creating a uniform look in the living room. The coffee table was a prototype for designer India Mahdavi, Anne's former employer. The geometric rug by Lindell & Co carries the same teal, as well as an unexpected shot of green.

OPPOSITE

The third-floor living room benefits from lovely light flowing through the huge windows and illuminating the teal paint. At night, the room takes on a rich moodiness by lamplight. The abundance of blue is punctuated by black accessories and artwork. The chaise longue originally belonged to Anne's mother.

RIGHT

On the top floor, part of the roof terrace was enclosed to create a small seating area and a bijou kitchen in which to prepare meals to eat on the terrace. It's a deceptively simple look – concrete floors, vivid green paint and potted plants. The sleek black daybed was customized to fit the space by removing one set of legs.

In Montmartre – that most Parisian of Paris neighbourhoods – Anne and husband Guillaume Juherian, a director of documentaries, share a beautifully bold home with their daughters Leia, aged 15, and Colette, 10, and Plume the cat. When they bought the property five years ago, it was divided into four apartments. The couple spent a year redesigning and rebuilding the four-storey space to suit the needs of their young family, retaining only the original staircase. The house is wider than it is deep, so rather than carve up the space further, most of the floors are open plan, maximizing the width and enhancing the depth of the interior with clever visual tricks.

What Anne does so well, both at home and in her design practice Double G with partner Flora de Gastines,

OPPOSITE
On the ground floor, the large kitchen/dining room
is fantastically bold in a clean and considered way.
Thanks to a tight colour story of black, white, blue
and mustard, the space doesn't feel overwhelming,
despite the Mosaic del Sur encaustic tiles that line
the wall between the pantry cupboards – a brilliant
way to create an interesting feature without
introducing another element. The paper pendants
are by Paola Navone for Monoprix, but you could
make your own with plain ones and a marker pen.

is strike a balance between the use of colour
and pattern. Anne has created a luxe home
from some fairly basic materials. Her trick?
Paint and restraint. Her palette is limited
to inky blues, greens and greys (with the
exception of her youngest daughter's pink
room – it's hard to say no to a 10-year-old's
request for pink), but when it comes to
application, Anne has really gone for it,
painting walls, cupboards, shelving and
window frames as well as adding a graphic
painted design to the stairwell walls.
Despite using strong patterns in the form
of wallpaper and textiles, Anne tempers them
with her restrained palette, and the result is
cool and sophisticated rather than garish.

The ground floor is one large open-plan
kitchen/dining room with doors that open
onto the garden – one of the features that
enticed the couple to move from their former
(gardenless) home. While Anne handles the
interiors, Guillame is all about the garden
and even grows his own vegetables. In the first
of many bold statements, Anne chose to cover
the floor in graphic tiles, extending some up
one wall. From here, climb the winding black

ABOVE LEFT & RIGHT
The interiors of the
kitchen cabinets have
been painted a rich blue,
against which a colourful
collection of crockery
stands out. Don't overlook
details like this – taking
that extra step makes
a room feel complete.
Why opt for plain white
tableware when you can
layer colourful patterned
china like this by India
Mahdavi for Monoprix?

LEFT & RIGHT

The master suite is serene, grounded by a soothing palette of blue, green and black. Solid-coloured linen was chosen for the bed, the only pattern here being the Cloudy wallpaper by Bien Fait. The curtains were made by adding small grommets to the top corners of fabric panels and hanging them on two hooks. When one corner is released, the fabric falls gracefully, letting in light.

LEFT

In the bedroom, deep blue geometric carpet – Escargot by Hartley & Tissier – is soft and comforting underfoot, but in the en-suite bathroom, polished concrete is more practical. Partially screened off by metal windows, the bathroom has a luxe hotel vibe. Matt black tiles cover the back wall – more sophisticated than glossy ones.

staircase and you find yourself on the girls' floor: two bedrooms, each with their own study nook and cleverly linked by an internal window. Colette's room has soft grey walls, a pale pink ceiling and oversized poppy-motif wallpaper. Rather than papering the entire wall, a simple wooden frame was built out around the bed, adding a sense of depth and offering another surface for paint, this time a dark pink to complement the wallpaper.

In Leia's room, colours are muted, with a fish-scale patterned wallpaper, graphic printed carpet and pops of colour in the shape of accessories. I've always been an advocate of allowing kids to personalize their rooms, particularly teenagers, who are often desperate to express their individuality. My mum let me draw on my walls, and Anne has allowed Leia to doodle on her lacquered green bedside table. Details like these give a home its personality.

Be BOLD

Children's rooms are a good excuse to have fun with patterned wallpaper. If you avoid designs that are overly juvenile, they should have longevity, carrying little ones through to the teenage years. These prints are dramatic, but work well with other colours and patterns.

Above the girls' floor is the master suite, which is again mostly open plan – a trend I'm seeing more and more with en-suite bedrooms. Sticking to her palette of blues and greens, Anne has covered one wall in wallpaper featuring pointillist clouds, a calming choice in a sea of bold colour. One more flight of stairs and you reach the living room, which has high ceilings, parquet floors, a wall of windows and some seriously good furniture. The walls, bookshelves, chaise longue (once belonging to Anne's mother) and velvet sofa are all the same shade of blue. It's a clever trick and creates a cosy, cocoon-like atmosphere in what could be a cavernous space.

At the very top of the house, the couple have enclosed part of what had been a terrace, adding a small kitchen for summertime meals on the roof. Painted bright green and minimally decorated with just a daybed and potted plants, it's the perfect place to settle in with a book, the cat and, if you crane your head, a view of Sacre Coeur.

LEFT

In 15-year-old Leia's room, wallpaper with a fan-shaped pattern covers the walls. The bed sits directly on the floor, its rattan frame matching the chair (the perfect spot for discarded clothes). The busy wallpaper is calmed by the freshness of various shades of blue and green, including the glossy bedside table/night stand that's been 'decorated' by Leia with a marker pen.

OPPOSITE

Ten year-old Colette's room is unmistakably feminine, the only pop of pink in the entire house. Oversized poppies cover the walls by the bed, the wallpaper set within a wooden frame to create more impact. Star-print curtain panels and a geometric carpet clash unabashedly, but are balanced by the plain linen bedding.

Fantasy FACTORY

A creative pair have breathed new life into this rundown former munitions factory in the middle of the woods. It's situated a short drive northeast of Amsterdam's city centre in Hembrugterrein, Zaandam, once an industrial area and the heart of the Dutch military, but now a thriving hub of culture, design and entrepreneurship.

ABOVE LEFT & RIGHT
A smart and simple kitchen island has been crafted from basic materials in the large open-plan area. The unit is made from grey-painted fibreglass, slim copper piping is used for the water spout and drawer pulls, and the taps/faucets are inexpensive industrial-style valves.

OPPOSITE
Many of the property's raw finishes have been left exposed, a nod to the building's history as well as a money-saving option. Flaking doors, stairs and walls are in stark contrast to the newly poured concrete floors and the rich tobacco paint applied part-way up the walls.

My favourite part of making a book is seeing all the different ways in which people create a home. I've seen some unusual places over the course of my career, but this was a first. Interior and product designer Tjimkje de Boer and her business partner Michiel Post have set up shop in a huge brick building that was once an ammunition depot. Set in almost 100 acres of wooded land, it is surrounded by similar buildings at varying stages of renovation, many occupied by entrepreneurs like them. It's part of an initiative to revitalize the area, and as designers looking for more space for less money, Tjimkje and Michiel were lured here from the city in 2016. As the crow flies, they are about 7km/4m from Amsterdam and Tjimkje can cycle to a ferry and be in the city in 10 minutes.

The majority of the building is a studio and workshop for the pair. Downstairs is a vast open space used as a showroom, with a handful of doors leading off to workshops, offices and storage spaces. To the right is the kitchen area, a long fibreglass island painted grey and fitted with a sink and a hob/stovetop. There is no furniture and the only decoration is the rich tobacco paint that extends halfway up the walls, leaving much of the original flaking plasterwork exposed.

The extra-long kitchen island, concrete floor and fresh coat of paint on the lower part of the wall were all added by Tjimkje and Michiel. These inexpensive updates to the old factory have elevated the space into one worthy of displaying the pair's designs, including their sound-absorbing Acoustic lights, seen here.

LEFT AND OPPOSITE
With so much going on in this open-plan space, the use of untreated wood offers welcome respite from the clash of colours. Tjimkje made the sliding door (left) from wooden planks arranged in a 3D graphic design.

Hanging above the island are designs from the pair's acoustic lighting range. Made from melamine absorption foam, these huge, undulating pendant lights are designed to absorb sound as well as make a design statement. Also on display are Tjimkje's Picturesque mirrors, each one made by hand from mirror glass and coloured epoxy.

Climb the wooden stairs and to the right, taking up most of the upper floor, is more work space: huge tables with prototype lights in various stages of completion, plus tools, dust and paint. This is a proper working studio where ideas germinate and bloom. But to the left of the stairs is a large wooden sliding door.

RIGHT
Tjimkje made this screen from salvaged doors found on the property and elsewhere. Behind it she stashes various bits she would prefer not to have on show. A screen like this can double as a backdrop to display your prettier pieces of clothing (or, let's be honest, the clothes you've tried on and haven't yet put away).

Be BOLD

What better way to make a bold statement than with a graphic 'rug' painted on the floor? Here, the floorboards were already in need of refinishing, but rather than face the task of updating the entire floor, one area was given special treatment with tough floor paint. Tjimkje designed this using a computer programme, but you can also buy ready-made stencils.

BELOW

No less than six paint colours were used on the loft walls, a different candy-coloured shade filling each pie-shaped slice created by the wooden framework. The exposed architecture has become part of the room's design, its beams and posts creating varying shapes and angles depending on where you stand.

OPPOSITE

In the bedroom end of the loft, a calmer mood is evoked with soothing peachy pink shades on the walls and a large white textured canvas behind the bed. A raised platform has been created by grouping shipping palettes together, the excess around the edges becoming a useful shelf.

Enter, and it's as if you're in a completely different building. This area has been partitioned off and converted into a boldly decorated apartment by Tjimkje. With little more than wood and paint, she has created a joyful hideaway tucked away in the eaves. It is open plan, with a simple wooden framework creating a sense of separation between the different areas. To the right is a dining area and to the left is the living room, with a black and white 'rug' painted on the floor. Next to this is Tjimkje's bedroom, where her clothes hang on a rail and all the unsightly stuff – boxes, wet suits, brooms – is hidden discreetly behind a screen she made from old doors.

The space is decorated minimally with furniture Tjimkje inherited from her parents and grandparents, as well as salvaged pieces and some designer bits. Tying it all together is glorious, saturated colour. The bedroom is all rich peachy pinks and flashes of mustard, while in the living area two shades of green pack a powerful punch alongside the acid yellow sofa. Tempered by the abundance of plywood, chipboard and pine, Tjimkje's imaginative use of paint doesn't assault the senses. Her colours are bright but muted, rich yet soft – a deliciously juicy palette that energizes but doesn't overstimulate.

OPPOSITE & RIGHT
Kitchens are often painted in neutral colours as a safe option, but Zoë and Gavin went all-out bold in their kitchen extension with electric blue paint. They also introduced pattern in the form of Moroccan tiles, installed by Gavin in a deliberately imperfect manner for added character. The storage containers are by Grace Souky and the pendant is Tom Dixon.

ABOVE RIGHT
Stems of fabulous 'faux-liage', as Zoë calls her fake flowers, are arranged in a blue vintage ceramic vase alongside a pair of vibrant blue candles and blue Jonathan Adler ceramics. Don't be afraid to colour-block accessories in this way – it's bold and calming at the same time.

Your home
IS YOUR CANVAS

Zoë Anderson and I have a mutual friend and whenever I met up with her she would say "You *have* to meet Zoë. You guys would get along." Eventually we did meet, the three of us enjoying cocktails and tapas in a local restaurant, and of course Zoë and I hit it off. When I sent a message to friends and family saying I was looking for bold homes for my new book, whose name should come up but Zoë's.

With a background in advertising and a passion for fashion and interiors, Zoë's home is filled with beautifully clashing colours and an effortlessly cool and layered style that has developed over the years.

On a quiet residential street in North London's Finsbury Park, Zoë shares her late-Victorian home with husband Gavin, daughter Ruby Blue, 17, and cat Odd (who once had a feline sidekick called Socks).

Gavin is global managing director of an advertising agency and Zoë runs W.A. Green, an independent interiors shop she set up in 2017 in London's Shoreditch. The family moved into the house in 2003, when Ruby was two and their son Sonny was three. In 2011 they lost Sonny to cancer. He was just 11 years old. Despite going through the most unimaginably horrific experience a family can face, their home is a warm and welcoming place, a cosy cocoon brimming with love, happiness and cherished memories. Family photos line the entryway and mementos of family life are dotted throughout. Children's drawings are framed and hung with pride alongside artwork by

OPPOSITE
The blue walls are a vibrant backdrop for the family's art collection and the Tom Dixon copper pendant light. Zoë and Gavin are avid art collectors and particularly enjoy supporting up-and-coming artists. Sharing wall space with artists' works are drawings by the children and keepsakes collected on the couple's travels, all hung salon style.

RIGHT
The blue paint in the conservatory-style kitchen draws you in from the cosy cocoon-like living room, which is painted in a dark grey-green. Design classics like the Eames Eiffel chairs sit around the dining table, but Zoë likes to mix in vintage from different eras, like the red rug, the glass ceiling light and the floor lamp, all purchased at various antiques markets and shops in London.

ABOVE LEFT
Accessorizing the
extra-long Ligne Roset
sofa are cushions by
Silken Favours. On the
wall, a huge painting
by Florence Blanchard
represents pills viewed
through a kaleidoscope.

ABOVE RIGHT
The simple beauty of a
child's handprint becomes
a breathtaking piece of
art when enlarged and
framed. This is Sonny's
handprint, made by his
intensive-care nurse and
cherished by the family.

heavyweights like Damien Hirst and younger artists such as Florence
Blanchard. Meticulously built Lego models – many of them made
by Sonny during his frequent hospital stays – share shelf space with
ceramics by Jonathan Adler and Atelier Stella. It's the eclectic, effortless
and experimental vibe that makes this a real home.

After 15 years' worth of memories, the couple feel this is probably
their forever home and now approach furniture purchases with more
care, thinking in terms of pieces that will stand the test of time. In their
flat-hopping days pre-kids, cheaper items featured heavily, but now
Zoë and Gavin have found the right balance between waiting patiently
to purchase investment pieces and indulging in impulse buys, then
finding a way of making them work. Zoë says she agonized over the
colour of their Ligne Roset sofa, knowing they would have it for years
to come. They even had to permanently seal one of the doors to the
living room to fit it in. But instead of playing it safe when it comes to
expensive items, they go for bold, as demonstrated by the lemon velvet
armchair, also by Ligne Roset, the jade and brass ombre cabinet by
Bethan Gray and the apple green, custom-made velvet curtains.

OPPOSITE
Zoë professes to dress
her home rather like she
dresses herself: in simple
pieces with loads of
accessories. Nowhere is
this more evident than
in the living room, where
furniture is upholstered
in three different velvets,
with personality and
pattern introduced via
cushions, artworks and
accessories. Heavy green
velvet curtains throw yet
another colour into the
stylish mix.

PAGES 114 & 115
In the master bedroom, one wall is covered in paisley Cole & Son wallpaper, while the rest is painted a greeny grey. The decadent silk satin eiderdown and cushions are by Preen. Facing the bed is an ornate metal fireplace turned into a display of plants, perfume, jewellery and outfits that Zoë is planning for upcoming events. A shrine to style – and no fashion shrine would be complete without a vintage *Vogue* cover, this one blown up and framed.

LEFT
Ruby's room is just how a teenager's bedroom should be: a self-decorated, evolving space in which to express herself. The matt black walls and door are a striking choice and perfect for displaying her collection of photos. On the bed is a throw by Slowdown Studio, and cushions by Silken Favours and Bella Freud.

Be **BOLD** ➝

Installing a large-scale mosaic is a serious commitment. But that one piece can work miracles, taking a room from blah to bold. Zoë and Gavin had this Bisazza mosaic installed when they moved in and love it to this day. The wall colour and accessories have changed over the years, but the bold black floral continues to make a statement.

It is this confidence with interiors, a passion for ever-changing fashion and her boredom with the minimalist, pared-back edits on offer in London's interiors scene that first sparked Zoë's idea for W.A. Green. A homewares store bursting with colour, happiness and fun, it is a maximalist's dream and the company's slogan – 'Dopamine for the home' – says it all. For Zoë, the line between her shop and her home is blurred, each one influencing the other. Both mix high and low – luxury furniture by established brands cohabits effortlessly with artwork by up-and-coming artists, and colours that aren't supposed to work together make sense simply because Zoë says they do. The over-arching feeling you get from both spaces is that life is fleeting, so enjoy every moment.

ABOVE LEFT

On a shelf in the bathroom, a collection of cheeky Jonathan Adler ceramic jars stores bathroom necessities without sacrificing style. The black terracotta candlesticks are by **DAY** Birger et Mikkelsen and look great with the neon candles. Don't overlook the impact a few special pieces can have in the bathroom.

ABOVE LEFT

Pien searched for a ceramic tiger for years, eventually finding a seller on Marktplaats, a Dutch online marketplace similar to eBay/Gumtree/Craigslist. He stands guard near the back door, sometimes getting dressed up with scarves. The painted wardrobe/armoire in the background is from Van Dijk en Ko in Amsterdam.

OPPOSITE & ABOVE RIGHT

Pien inherited the 1940s Gispen table by Christoffel Hoffmann from her grandmother, who once used it as a cutting table in her fabric shop. The leather dining chairs are by Dutch brand Jess Design, while the copper pendant lights are by British designer Tom Dixon.

Into the
WILD

I love being surprised by a home. Nothing delights me more than entering a building that, from the outside, seems rather unassuming, only to discover a treasure trove hidden within its walls. In the Dutch city of Zwolle, behind the doors of a brick townhouse built in 1919, such delights await thanks to the creativity of its owner, Pien Essink.

Pien and her husband Rick, general manager of a trailer company, bought the three-storey house in early 2016. A mere two years later, they have converted it into a stylish and practical family home in which to raise their two young sons Kees and Dorus, aged six and four. The interior demonstrates that a bold home doesn't require orange walls, zigzag-painted floors and clashing patterns. It can also have a neutral backdrop enlivened with pops of strong colour and daring furniture and accessories – something Pien and Rick have done so well.

Pien studied in Zwolle for four years before continuing her studies at Eindhoven's renowned Design Academy. She went on to work for Dutch brand Pip Studio, spending seven years designing patterns for everything from wallpaper to teapots. Now she has ventured out on her own, designing for various companies as well as building her own brand, Studio Pien. Pien is one of those creative people who are difficult to categorize. She does it all – styling, visual merchandizing, photography and surface design. Because of her many talents, Pien's home has a playful style, a look that is effortless and not to be taken too seriously.

The ground floor is light and airy with poured concrete floors, clean white walls and a pleasing

OPPOSITE & ABOVE
In the living room, a fearlessly bold combination of colours and patterns are grounded by the pink velvet sofa and linked by a felt wall hanging that Pien purchased online. The large stripes of the rug offset the smaller prints on the cushions, one of which proves that leopard print goes with everything.

The clean lines of the white and wood kitchen are brought to life with shots of colour and an ever-changing display of the kids' artwork. The stools were bought second-hand and cut down to fit the counter height. The decanter pendant lights are by Lee Broom.

collection of junk-shop finds, contemporary pieces and family heirlooms. This is the part of the house where the couple invested the most, removing a false ceiling, reconfiguring the space into a spacious open-plan living and eating space and adding smooth concrete flooring, perfect for the activities of two young children (bikes, skateboards, balls…). The kitchen is modern, stylish and efficient. Its white and wood finishes are enhanced by Pien's second-hand finds – the metal tiger on the wall was once in a

zoo, and the red metal and velvet stools were found on Dutch online classifieds site Markplaats (a cross between eBay, Gumtree and Craigslist), Pien's favourite place to hunt for unusual bargains.

At the front of the house in the living room, an unlikely collection of furniture and accessories comes together perfectly. I love this space and the combination of a pale pink sofa with a graphic black and white striped rug. But for me, what makes this room extra special and takes it from 'mainstream bold' to 'eclectic, personality-filled bold' is the artful layering of seemingly mismatched elements – a felt wall hanging, green and gold velvet pouffes, marble-topped side tables and red embroidered and leopard-print cushions. The pink, gold and green in the wall hanging tie the scheme together, but the addition of mismatched cushions gives the room the off-kilter finish that I love so much.

OPPOSITE
On the second floor Pien has her home studio. An IKEA dining table serves as her desk, allowing more space to spread out. Mementos from her travels adorn the sapphire-painted wall.

ABOVE
The stairs are a showstopper in egg yolk yellow, the cheerful hue bouncing off the white walls and casting a sunny warmth throughout. In the office, Pien added neon washi tape to the edges of some old floral paintings for an easy modern update.

RIGHT
Pien stapled a black and white sheet to her headboard – an easy revamp if you tire of the upholstery. Stripes work with practically everything, including this felt wall hanging. The IKEA reading lights are simply clipped into place.

LEFT & ABOVE

Floral designs, polka dots and insects all get along beautifully here. Different patterns mix seamlessly when you balance large- and small-scale designs and stick to a limited palette – here blue, red and white. Pien designed the insect wallpaper when she worked at Pip Studio. The red box and shelf are souvenirs from her travels.

From the ground floor you are led upstairs on carpet reminiscent of Dorothy's yellow brick road. The egg yolk hue is an exciting alternative to safe beige, and when offset with cool white walls and whitewashed floorboards, it works brilliantly. The rest of the house displays the same juxtaposition of bright colour and neutral bases: plywood floors and wallpaper designed by Pien in the boys' rooms, and blue and burgundy paint and white floorboards in Pien's office. Only in the master bedroom did she opt for a calmer palette, although a striped headboard and another felt wall hanging keep it in sync with the rest of the home.

Pien and Rick have discovered a way to bring bold elements into their home without overwhelming the senses. They have found that sweet spot where old and new, colourful and muted, and bold and calm meet. And with Pien constantly creating, I imagine the space won't stay the same for long, with furniture and accessories always in flux.

 **BOLD**

Feeding the imagination during childhood nurtures the next generation of big bold dreamers. And what better way to do that than a mural? Think of the hours spent lying in bed, every day finding something new in this whimsical scene. Pien designed it for her son Kees, even including his name in the mural.

THIS PAGE & OPPOSITE
Organic materials and feminine touches soften
the industrial architecture of the apartment. The
huge custom-made dining table was created by
slotting together slabs of marble and beautifully
textured wood, jigsaw style. One corner has been
fitted with banquette seating, upholstered in
Martineau, a jacquard velvet by Designers Guild,
while a stylishly quirky collection of mismatched
chairs provides additional seating. A huge glossy
photo in the style of a Dutch Master's still-life
painting completes the look.

Punk Rock
BAROQUE

On the sixth floor of a former printworks in Paris, designer
Laura Gauthier Petit and her husband Pascal, a restaurateur,
have created a luxurious penthouse that is part-punk,
part-Belle Époque, the two cleverly blended against an
industrial setting that boasts panoramic views of the city.

The couple spent two years renovating the apartment with the help of friend, designer and architect Olivier Gay. They had been searching for a home in the city's third arrondissement to be near son Maël's school, but were losing hope as everything was either too expensive or just not right. A friend tipped them off about a building that was being rebuilt by a developer and they managed to get in for a sneak peek before the work was complete.

With a rooftop boasting a 360-degree view of Paris, the apartment was a rare find and one they couldn't pass up.

Laura works in fashion, heading up her own couture label Fête Impériale, which she founded in 2015, but her design talents clearly extend to interiors as well. In fact, she also helped with the interiors of ISTR, the oyster restaurant her husband co-owns. Like many fashion designers, Laura's home is an extension of her

ABOVE
A cluster of planters-cum-pendant lights hangs above the marble-topped kitchen island. These are the Well Planter Light by Object/Interface, but there are more affordable options available. Plant them with herbs for easy access when cooking.

RIGHT
At one end of the open-plan kitchen/ dining room, a mural covers the entire wall. Surface View sells similar styles and will custom print to fit your space. Oversized lighting and a taxidermied albino peacock add a contemporary spin to the pastoral scene. The Muffin lamp is by Brokis, but you can find similar tripod lamps at Made.com.

OPPOSITE
Ceiling-height windows divide the kitchen from the living room, offering a sense of separation while maintaining a view through the interior. Ductwork has been left exposed, in keeping with the industrial spirit of the apartment.

fashion sense – the two are inseparable. At Fête Impériale she doesn't care to follow the rules, and the same can be said of her interiors style. The Gauthier Petit home earns its Bold badge by combining contrasting styles and finishes that are usually at odds with one another.

The basic shell of the apartment is industrial in style, with concrete beams, ductwork and steel support columns on show. Not exactly a nurturing environment for a family, so Laura set to work adding touches of softness throughout. Every room has had a vivid injection of colour and pattern, a feminine flourish to contrast with the hard surfaces. These are confident choices, not just a flowery cushion here and there. Entire walls

OPPOSITE
An oversized modular Roche Bobois sofa in grey leather dominates one end of the living room. It is a luxurious addition to the space, but is made more family friendly by the scattering of eclectic cushions. The Light Forest ceiling lights are by Ontwerpduo for &Tradition.

ABOVE RIGHT
The oversized theme continues with a round sofa covered in purple velvet, part of the Amoenus collection by Antonio Citterio for Maxalto. Cut-outs in the partition wall allow light to filter in from the roof terrace above.

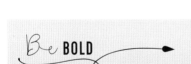
Be BOLD

Break from tradition by layering unexpected, contrasting materials. Glossy metro tiles are an unconventional choice for a living room, but look striking when sealed with black grout and hung on the diagonal. Heavily textured velvet jacquard curtains make a strong statement in contrast to the white tiled wall and parquet flooring.

are upholstered in botanical fabrics, bathroom walls are tiled with mosaics, curtains are made from velvet brocades.

Boldness is introduced not only by these self-assured strokes of brilliance but also through Laura's choice of furniture and lighting. It's one of those homes where nothing has been overlooked. Every detail has been considered, from the oversized Roche Bobois sofa to the &Tradition lighting to the mismatched dining chairs, each one fabulously quirky but still luxe.

In my experience, when the budget goes up, creativity often goes down. If it's easy to buy whatever you want, you don't have to be as resourceful … and resourcefulness usually leads to creativity. But I will admit that this is not the case here. Yes, there are some fabulous, not-so-budget-friendly designer pieces dotted throughout, but there are also some inventive ideas that give this home its personality. A few standouts are the custom-made dining table, crafted from pieces of wood and marble slotted together like a giant jigsaw (an idea that could be copied with less expensive materials and the help of a carpenter), the metro tile laid diagonally on the living room walls and overlaid with velvet brocade curtains and the brightly upholstered wardrobe/closet doors partnered with wild pink palm leaf carpet in Laura's dressing room.

These are gutsy choices, entirely fitting for a family led by a strong woman who is a self-professed non-conformist. Laura's quirky, feminine and luxurious spin on bold style resonates through both her home and her clothing collections, and is a reminder that our home should reflect all the facets of our personality, no matter how much we might think they clash.

OPPOSITE

The simplest way to a bold bedroom is a statement wallpaper. When you dare to use the wildest of patterns, little else is needed. Here, a kaleidoscopic tile-effect paper covers the entire wall and is accessorized with a vintage ceiling light and pieces of amber glass.

ABOVE

In the master bathroom, Laura has married baroque decadence and sleek modernity. The luxurious double-width black Organico bathtub is by Spanish designer Jaime Hayon. For the wall, Patricia Urquiola's Jardin Rouge mosaic is an unflinchingly confident choice. Concrete floor tiles and a slice of pink palm leaf carpet complete the look.

FAR LEFT & LEFT
An ultramarine and brass
theme is first introduced
in the entryway, then
continues throughout the
ground floor. The black
and white tiles are by
Popham Design and the
teardrop-shaped brass
wall lights are from Italian
brand Fuoriluogo Design.

Naturally
BOLD

About half an hour northwest of Paris, in the quiet town of Vernouillet,
Priscilla and Guillame have exported a slice of cool city living to the leafy
suburbs in the form of their relaxed and stylish family home. In 2016, the
couple traded a trendy neighbourhood in the centre of Paris for a quieter
life closer to their families. Now that they are parents to toddler Issa and
newborn Yanis, the importance of space and proximity to nature are of
greater relevance than ever before.

OPPOSITE
In the living room, an eclectic collection
of furniture is unified by the brass and
ultramarine theme. The organic colours
and textures of the different sofas
juxtapose with the graphic hand-painted
mural. Ceiling lights are by Markslöjd;
the wall lights by AMPM at La Redoute.

Be BOLD

In the dining room, more definitely means more. The wall that divides the kitchen and the dining area has had a coat of vibrant ultramarine paint for an extra bold pop. When layered with textured wallpaper by Pierre Frey and a large eye-shaped rattan mirror, it becomes softer and earthier. The look is completed by a huge Gervasoni brass pendant light.

RIGHT

In the home office, sheets of batik-print paper from Le Monde Sauvage have been applied to one section of the wall. You could do the same with handmade sheets from an art supply shop, fixing them in place with wallpaper glue. Applying individual sheets by hand gives a more imperfect hand-crafted finish.

Priscilla and Guillaume's new home was built in the 1980s and when they bought it hadn't been updated since that time. It sits within a huge garden, lush with palm, fig and chestnut trees, and has the luxury of an outdoor swimming pool.

With the help of interior designer Rebecca Kierszbaum, the couple completely renovated and furnished the house, remaining heavily involved in every step of the process. Despite having the help of an expert, the two-storey home doesn't feel overly designed – the vibe is natural and relaxed, testament to Rebecca's talent for designing for the client, not for herself. At 200sqm/2150sqft, it is a good-sized home for a family of four.

This is a great example of a home that is undeniably bold but not overwhelming.

The colour palette incorporates black, white, ultramarine and gold, and with the addition of old and new furniture and accessories in organic materials, the effect is quirky, eclectic and very personal. Downstairs, a low mango wood coffee table; chairs, side tables and a mirror all in rattan; and dining chairs printed with colourful patterns and textured wallpapers were all selected to contrast with the bolder, more graphic elements.

ABOVE

These dining room shelves have been painted inside with the same ultramarine paint, an easy trick for adding finesse to typically forgotten areas. The mesh doors were customized with glass beads.

ABOVE RIGHT & OPPOSITE

In the kitchen, glossy textured black tiles by Emery et Cie reflect light on the floor. Above, black IKEA cabinets, polished concrete countertops, textured white tiles and navy blue paint offer a sleek backdrop for the graphic stacking chairs and wooden table.

The walls are mostly light in colour, except for a vibrant shot of ultramarine blue on the wall dividing the kitchen from the dining area – a colour that reappears throughout the living areas in small doses. Black also plays its part, seen in the kitchen cabinets, woodwork/trim, slices of walls and the Popham Design tiles in the entryway.

In the living room, Rebecca came up with the idea of a hand-painted mural that stretches the length of the wall and incorporates the key colours of the palette – black, white, ultramarine and gold. The asymmetrical design breaks up a long expanse of wall and adds interest without being overpowering. The choice

of bronze velvet for the sofa was an excellent one – almost but not quite a neutral, it adds an earthiness that softens the graphic quality of the mural and contrasts beautifully with the glossy brass lighting.

Statement lights appear throughout, some small, some huge, all fantastic. Good lighting can transform a space, a concept these guys fully grasp. Even the entryway – a space often overlooked – has been given special treatment with a striking group of Italian brass lights that appear to drip down one wall like molten blobs of gold. The brass theme is continued throughout the house, with smaller directional lights near the sofa

In the bedroom, a floating wall was installed to conceal the dressing area and bark-effect wallpaper by Elitis was applied to one side. A fine balance has been struck between solid colour and soft pattern. The natural tones and textures create a peaceful environment for relaxation without being dull.

Nature is at the core of the master suite's design, so birch tree trunks were chosen to divide the bedroom and bathroom, a motif that's echoed in the bedroom wallpaper. The natural imperfections in the handmade black tiles from Emery et Cie prevent the bathroom from appearing too slick.

and the beds and, of course, the dramatic Gervasoni pendant over the dining table.

We all know about the statement wall, but here the concept has been given a twist. In the dining room and master bedroom, sections of painted wall remain to the left and right of a panel of wallpaper; and in the office, paper has been applied to the lower section of one wall only. Aside from looking more interesting, it's also a gentler approach to being bold (with the added bonus of costing less, too).

Thoughtfully chosen furniture, statement features, a controlled colour palette and a careful balance between graphic and organic elements are what make this home a success, proving that bold doesn't have to mean brash.

OPPOSITE

In the dining room, Anna's painterly brushstrokes adorn every surface: walls, ceiling, furniture, picture frames, lampshades and ceramics. The copper paint on the ceiling creates a warm glow when lit by candlelight on a winter's night. A length of fabric from Anna's collection makes a unique tablecloth.

ABOVE LEFT & RIGHT

A few years back, Anna tried her hand at producing ceramics. The beautifully wonky finishes and hand-painted designs make them truly one of a kind. I would snap them up if she decided to offer them as part of her collection again!

Artist in RESIDENCE

In the two years since they moved in, Anna and Christopher Hayman have transformed their 1920s cottage in the English countryside into a decadent and bohemian feast for the eyes. By layering richly patterned fabric and wallpaper and covering almost every surface in hand-painted details, they have created an atmospheric home where Bloomsbury meets Biba.

The couple bought the cottage in the summer of 2016 from owners who had lived there for more than 40 years and had preserved its character. It was originally built for workers on the nearby Glynde Estate and retains many period features, including fireplaces, picture rails and Crittall windows. Very little work was required, aside from cosmetic touches, especially as the Haymans' goal was not to modernize but simply revitalize the cottage's 1920s style while giving it a modern edge. Conveniently, Anna is a talented pattern designer, creating original artwork for her own line of wallpapers, fabric, cushions and fringed lampshades, and testing her new ideas at home before they go up on her website.

In nearby Lewes, Anna has a studio from which she runs her business, Anna Hayman Designs. Like many female entrepreneurs, she juggles work with raising her two children,

LEFT
The kitchen is a great example of working with what you've got to make a home your own. Without undertaking a costly and disruptive overhaul, the couple have managed to make their mark with paint, tile and simple shelving while still preserving the cottage's spirit. Anna's own designs can be seen in the single panel of wallpaper, the splashback tiles and the linoleum prints.

Harrison and Spencer, aged eight and five, and structures her day around their school schedules. Christopher is a child psychotherapist and the couple have lived in the area for many years. But although they love country life, their home is not decorated in typical rustic style.

Instead, Anna has drawn inspiration from two of her favourite eras, the 1920s and 1960s. Nods to the Bloomsbury Set's East Sussex home Charleston Farmhouse are everywhere, with hand-painted flourishes adorning walls, door frames and furniture in a loose, naïve style. But the moody yet glamorous palette is straight out of Barbara Hulanicki's Biba, the coolest place to shop in 1960s London (my mum still goes starry-eyed when she reminisces about shopping there). The design of Biba was itself a reinvention of the golden age of the Art Deco period, so Anna has reinvented a reinvention!

OPPOSITE & RIGHT

Stepping into the living room is like stepping back in time. The 1920s mood of the room is evident in the colours and patterns as well as the style of the furniture. The warm and earthy palette of terracotta, aquamarine and gold was inspired by the sofa – a lucky eBay find and the first piece the pair bought for the house. The plaster finish on the walls was discovered beneath woodchip and given a wash to seal it. The blue-green paint on the chimney breast is a blend of three different paints and the brick fireplace surround is painted gold. The framed panel that hangs behind the sofa was painted by Anna in her signature style.

BELOW

A stool has been covered with velvet designed by Anna. She paints all her original designs, then prints them onto fabric for cushions, lampshades and furnishing fabric by the metre.

The first thing you see when you enter is the staircase leading up to the first floor. The treads have been covered with one of Anna's own wallpapers, with roughly painted lines of gold paint flanking each panel, and a chalky peach paint on the walls. The woodwork is painted black with gold lines brushed on freehand for a unique effect. To your left is the dining room, to the right the sitting room and behind lies the kitchen, leading onto the large garden. The dining room is dark and glamorous in an Art Deco fashion. Teal walls are dotted with small gold crosses and Anna has painted trompe l'oeil panelling on one wall in black, white and gold. I can imagine how fabulous it must look by candlelight, with the flames catching the crosses and the gold ceiling (did I mention the gold ceiling?)

Be BOLD

Indulge in a passion for pattern by layering various designs in a similar colour palette. In her bedroom, Anna has created a decadent and glamorous sanctuary filled with her favourite printed silks and velvets. She has varied the scale of each design – large-scale pattern on the walls and smaller prints on the cushions.

LEFT

In her son's bedroom, bold style gets a playful twist. One of Anna's wallpapers provides a hit of pattern, but rather than paper the entire room in the dizzyingly fun design, only a section of the wall has been covered. A richly hued antique wooden cabinet displays Lego models and prized toy cars.

OPPOSITE

The rest of the room is painted a powdery blue, a calming choice punctuated by vivid textiles. The London bus bedding is a perfect choice for a child's room.

More of Anna's painterly flourishes can be seen on chests of drawers, lampshades and ceramics (made by Anna when she was on a pottery kick) – even the underside of a faux animal skin, now draped on a cabinet. A woman after my own heart, Anna favours creativity over perfection, and the energy with which she has decorated her home is what makes it so interesting.

Upstairs, the master bedroom is dark and sybaritic in feel. Anna has lined the walls with opulent black and gold wallpaper, piled the bed high with cushions and hung a fringed lamp, all of them her own designs. My favourite touch is the curtain, made from a piece of gold leather with an uneven hem – a creative solution to the problem of how to cover the window.

Anna's home has become an extension of her business, an informal showroom where she can endlessly experiment with new designs. And every room has – quite literally – her stamp on it, with Anna Hayman cushions, rugs and lamps crowding the space, their patterns and colours clashing in the most deliciously decadent way.

Sources

Life Unstyled/Emily Henson
www.lifeunstyled.com
www.emilyhensonstudio.com
@lifeunstyled on Instagram/
Facebook/Twitter/Pinterest
*That's me, talking all things interiors, creativity
before consumption, embracing imperfection,
working with what you've got and plenty of
oversharing from my personal life.*

FLOORS AND WALLS

Bert & May
www.bertandmay.com
*Vintage-inspired encaustic tiles
in patterns both bold and subtle.*

Cole and Son
www.cole-and-son.com
*Innovative, beautiful and whimsical
wallpaper designs.*

Emery et Cie
www.emeryetcie.com
Stunning tiles, wallpapers, fabric and paint.

Farrow & Ball
www.farrow-ball.com
*A favourite in the industry, renowned for both
their range of colours and their chalky finish.*

Ligne Roset
www.ligne-roset.com
*Contemporary furniture with luxurious,
distinctive shapes and styles.*

Little Greene
www.littlegreene.com
*An extensive range of paint colours and
wallpaper designs. Their floor paint is tough,
washable and can be used on both wooden
and concrete floors.*

Lucy Tiffney
www.lucytiffneyshop.com
*Lucy hand-paints brilliantly bold
interpretations of natural elements for
her wallpaper and mural range.*

Popham Design
www.pophamdesign.com
*Cement tiles handmade in Morocco using
traditional techniques and bold, modern designs.*

Surface View
www.surfaceview.co.uk
*An incredible collection of images, all
customizable to fit your walls as a mural,
wallpaper, or wall hanging.*

FURNITURE/ACCESSORIES/ LIGHTING

Anna Hayman Designs
www.annahaymandesigns.com
*Lampshades, wallpaper, fabrics and rugs
with a decadent Biba-esque vibe.*

Anthropologie
www.anthropologie.com
*Floral sofas, bright velvet footstools,
geometric side tables – they've got it all.*

Beldi Rugs
www.beldirugs.com
*A beautifully curated collection of vintage
Moroccan rugs available online.*

Caravane
www.caravane.fr
*Furniture, lighting, colourful linens and
everything else for the home. French style
with a modern bohemian twist.*

Entler
www.entler.co
*A ceramic lighting studio based in Los Angeles.
Jonathan Entler designs curvy, organic,
futuristic lamps that would be at home in the
classic French children's book Barbapapa's
New House (an all-time fave of mine).*

Graham & Green
www.grahamandgreen.co.uk
*Family-run interiors shops selling an
eclectic mix of furniture and accessories.*

House of Hackney
www.houseofhackney.com
*An unashamedly maximalist brand putting
a modern spin on quintessentially British
patterns. Furniture, fabric, wallpaper and
accessories designed to be layered for a
quirky, luxurious look.*

Matthew Williamson
www.matthewwilliamson.com
*I love everything Matthew designs, but more
importantly I love the way he clashes patterns
and colours for an eclectic bohemian vibe.
Wallpapers, sofas, rugs, fabrics – he does it all.*

Pooky
www.pooky.com
*Affordable decorative lighting. A great
resource for their extensive collection of
printed and solid-coloured lampshades.*

Rockett St George
www.rockettstgeorge.co.uk
Quirky, daring and unexpected furnishings.

Slowdown Studio
www.slowdownstudio.com
*Blankets woven with designs by artists and
illustrators; they look great hung on a wall.*

Tom Dixon
www.tomdixon.net
*Bold, glamorous lighting in dramatic shapes
and finishes.*

W.A.Green
www.wagreen.co.uk
*Zoe Anderson stocks her East London store
with a wildly colourful, feel-good edit of
furniture, throws, cushions and ceramics.
Also available online.*

Wicklewood
www.wicklewood.com
*Ethically sourced designs for the home,
from cushions to rugs to vases.*

Picture credits

Endpapers Zoë Anderson; **1** The home of Pien Essink of Studio Pien, The Netherlands; **2** The home of Theo-Bert Pot (interior blogger and stylist The Nice Stuff Collector) and Jelle van de Schoor (interior architect) in The Hague; **3** The home of Amy Exton in Margate is available to hire at margatelocationhouse. com; **4** The family home of Chris and Rachel Roberts in London. House designed by architects Office S & M; **5 left and 5 right** Rebecca Kierszbaum for Kierszbaum Intérieurs; **5** The Madrid home of the interior designer Patricia Bustos de la Torre Instagram.com/patricia_bustos, www.patricia-bustos.com; **6** The home of Laura Gauthier founder and creative director of Fête Impériale, Paris; **7** Rebecca Kierszbaum for Kierszbaum Intérieurs; **8** The Madrid home of the interior designer Patricia Bustos de la Torre Instagram.com/patricia_bustos, www. patricia-bustos.com; **9** The home of Theo-Bert Pot (interior blogger and stylist The Nice Stuff Collector) and Jelle van de Schoor (interior architect) in The Hague; **10–11** Rebecca Kierszbaum for Kierszbaum Intérieurs; **12** The home of the designer Tjimkje de Boer of tjimkje.com; **13 above left** The family home of Chris and Rachel Roberts in London. House designed by architects Office S & M; **13 above right** The home of the designer Tjimkje de Boer of tjimkje.com; **13 below left** Anna Hayman www.annahaymandesigns.com; **15** The home of interior designer Anne Geistdoerfer and Guillaume Juheiran and their girls Leia and Colette; **16** The Madrid home of the interior designer Patricia Bustos de la Torre Instagram.com/ patricia_bustos, www.patricia-bustos.com; **17** The home of Amy Exton in Margate is available to hire margatelocationhouse.com; **18** Zoë Anderson; **19 above right** The home of Amy Exton in Margate is available to hire at margatelocationhouse.com; **19 below left** Rebecca Kierszbaum for Kierszbaum Intérieurs; **19 below centre** The family home of Chris and Rachel Roberts in London. House designed by architects Office S & M; **21** The home of Laura Gauthier founder and creative director of Fête Impériale, Paris; **22** The Madrid home of the interior designer Patricia Bustos de la Torre Instagram.com/patricia_bustos, www. patricia-bustos.com; **23** Rebecca Kierszbaum for Kierszbaum Intérieurs; **24 above** Anna Hayman www.annahaymandesigns. com; **24 below and 25** The home of interior designer Anne Geistdoerfer and Guillaume Juheiran and their girls Leia and Colette; **26** The home of Theo-Bert Pot (interior blogger and stylist The Nice Stuff Collector) and Jelle van de Schoor (interior architect) in The Hague; **27 above** Zoë Anderson; **27 below** The home of interior designer Anne Geistdoerfer and Guillaume Juheiran and their girls Leia and Colette; **28** Anna Hayman www.annahaymandesigns.com; **30 above** Rebecca Kierszbaum for Kierszbaum Intérieurs; **30 below** The home of Theo-Bert Pot (interior blogger and stylist The Nice Stuff Collector) and Jelle van de Schoor (interior architect) in The Hague; **31** The home of interior designer Anne Geistdoerfer and Guillaume Juheiran and their girls Leia and Colette; **32** The home of Pien Essink of Studio Pien, The Netherlands; **33** The home of Theo-Bert Pot (interior blogger and stylist The Nice Stuff Collector) and Jelle van de Schoor (interior architect) in The Hague; **34 left** The family home of Chris and Rachel Roberts in London. House designed by architects Office S & M; **34 right** The Madrid home of the interior designer Patricia Bustos de la Torre Instagram. com/patricia_bustos, www.patricia-bustos.com; **35** The home of Laura Gauthier of Fête Impériale, Paris; **36** The home of Pien Essink of Studio Pien, The Netherlands; **37** Rebecca Kierszbaum for Kierszbaum Intérieurs; **39** The home of Amy Exton in Margate is available to hire at margatelocationhouse.com; **40 and 41 above** Zoë Anderson; **41 below** The home of the designer Tjimkje de Boer of tjimkje.com; **42** Rebecca Kierszbaum for Kierszbaum Intérieurs; **43** The Madrid home of the interior designer Patricia Bustos de la Torre Instagram.com/patricia_ bustos, www.patricia-bustos.com; **44** The Madrid home of the interior designer Patricia Bustos de la Torre Instagram.com/ patricia_bustos, www.patricia-bustos.com; **45 left** The family home of Chris and Rachel Roberts in London. House designed by architects Office S & M; **45 right** Rebecca Kierszbaum for Kierszbaum Intérieurs; **46–57** The Madrid home of the interior designer Patricia Bustos de la Torre Instagram.com/patricia_ bustos, www.patricia-bustos.com; **58–67** The home of Theo-Bert Pot (interior blogger and stylist The Nice Stuff Collector) and Jelle van de Schoor (interior architect) in The Hague; **68–79** The home of Amy Exton in Margate is available to hire at margatelocationhouse.com; **80–89** The family home of Chris and Rachel Roberts in London House designed by architects Office S & M; **90–99** The home of interior designer Anne Geistdoerfer and Guillaume Juheiran and their girls Leia and Colette; **100–107** The home of the designer Tjimkje de Boer of tjimkje.com; **108–117** Zoë Anderson; **118–127** The home of Pien Essink of Studio Pien, The Netherlands; **128–135** The home of Laura Gauthier founder and creative director of Fête Impériale, Paris; **136–143** Rebecca Kierszbaum for Kierszbaum Intérieurs; **144–153** Anna Hayman www.annahaymandesigns.com; **155** The home of Laura Gauthier founder and creative director of Fête Impériale, Paris; **157** The home of Amy Exton in Margate is available to hire at margatelocationhouse.com; **160** The Madrid home of the interior designer Patricia Bustos de la Torre Instagram.com/patricia_bustos, www.patricia-bustos.com.

Business credits

Amy Exton
Set and Interior Design
E: amyextonlondon@gmail.com
E: amy@margatelocationhouse.com
www.margatelocationhouse.com
www.amyexton.com
Pages 3, 17, 19 above right, 39, 68–79.

Anna Hayman Designs
Unit 1/8 Phoenix House
33 North Street
Lewes
East Sussex BN7 2PH
www.annahaymandesigns.com
Pages 13 below left, 24 above, 28, 144–153.

Double g Interior Design
Anne Geistdoerfer and Flora
de Gastines
80 rue Saint Honoré
75001 Paris
T: +33 1 42 78 17 56
E: ecrire@doubleg.fr
www.doubleg.fr
Pages 15, 24 below, 25, 27 below, 31, 90–99.

Fête Impériale
28 rue du Roi de Sicile
75004 Paris
T: +33 1 57 40 69 30
www.feteimperiale.fr
Pages 6, 21, 35, 128–135.

Kierszbaum Intérieurs
E: info@kierszbaum-interieurs.com
www.kierszbaum-interieurs.com
*Pages 5 left, 5 right, 7, 10–11, 19 below left,
23, 30 above, 37, 42, 45 right, 136–143.*

Office S & M
18 Ashwin Street
London E8 3DL
T: +44 (0)20 3167 8791
E: office@officesandm.com
www.officesandm.com
*Pages 4, 13 above left, 19 below centre,
34 left, 45 left, 80–89.*

Patricia Bustos Studio
E: patricia@patricia-bustos.com
www.patricia-bustos.com
Instagram.com/patricia_bustos
*Pages 5 centre, 8, 16, 22, 34 right, 43, 44,
46–57, 160.*

Theo-Bert Pot
The Nice Stuff Collector
www.thenicestuffcollector.com
IG: theobert_pot
and
Jelle van de Schoor
Form Makers
www.formmakers.nl
Pages 2, 9, 26, 30 below, 33, 58–67.

Tjimkje de Boer
www.tjimkje.com
Tjimkje de Boer and Michiel Post
www.acousticdesignsolutions.com
Pages 12, 13 above right, 41 below, 100–107.

Studio Pien
Pien Essink
Freelance Designer
Zwolle
The Netherlands
T: +31 6 2426 7051
E: pien@studiopien.com
www.studiopien.com
instagram.com/studio_pien
Pages 1, 32, 36, 118–127.

W. A. Green
9–10 Charlotte Road
London EC2A 3DH
T: +44 (0)20 7729 8599
www.wagreen.co.uk
Pages 18, 27 above, 40, 41 above, 108–117.

Index

Page numbers in *italic* refer to the illustrations

Acknowledgments

I'm not going to lie – I didn't think there would be a fourth book. After *Modern Rustic*, *Bohemian Modern* and *Life Unstyled*, I thought I'd end it there. Three seemed like a good number – and my goodness, writing a book is hard work! Yet here we are with *Be Bold*, and I couldn't be happier. It seems I can't resist the pull of a new idea, inspiring homes and an excellent team. As always, my thanks go to the wonderful ladies of Ryland Peters & Small: Cindy Richards, for saying yes to another idea; Jess Walton, for helping me find the perfect mix of bold homes; my wonderful editor Annabel Morgan, who calmly helped me focus my thoughts and encouraged me to write with my own voice; Toni Kay, for her design skills; and Leslie Harrington, to whom I'm still indebted for asking me to pitch book ideas more than six years ago.

Reuniting with Catherine Gratwicke after working with her on my first book *Modern Rustic* was an absolute dream. Aside from being a brilliant photographer, she is a wonderful human being. We laughed our way across Europe, ate too many baguettes in Paris, walked on too many airport travellators and schemed silly future book titles.

Thank you to all the lovely homeowners who welcomed us into their homes and let us do our thing. I walked away from every shoot inspired by your homes and I'm grateful I can share them with my readers.

Thanks to all my loyal followers and readers, many of whom have been there since the early days of the Life Unstyled blog and now follow me on social media (@lifeunstyled). Your positive encouragement over the years is what keeps me going. Thank you!

Lastly, thanks to my family and friends, who have supported me over the last few years when times were tough, and who forgive me when I fall off the radar while making a book. And thanks to my children Ella and Johnny, who have grown into spectacular human beings. I dedicate this book to you.